Halogen

Recipes for use with you.

For Andrew & Sophie
My inspiration and motivation.
With love.

Contents

Halogen Heaven

"Until you get used to cooking with your Halogen Oven, you'll probably need a little bit of help, I know I did!

At first I wasn't sure whether food would be cooked enough or too well done; however after a few attempts and a little patience I haven't looked back.

Obviously I carefully studied the manufacturer's manual (and I suggest you do too!) but nothing beats simply having a go. I cooked everything I could possible think of; and so that you can cook all your favourites, I've put together this Halogen Oven cookbook to get you started!

The guide covers all types of meat and vegetables and can be used for both fresh and frozen food.

Not all the recipes in this guide and cookbook need fancy ingredients; in fact I hope that you'll find that your Halogen Oven is perfect for every occasion. Whether you want to make a quick snack or a full Sunday roast, there are lots of recipes to help you get to Halogen Heaven..."

Maryanne

About Halogen Ovens

A Halogen oven is a compact table top cooker which cooks food quickly and is healthier than traditional cooking methods. It uses powerful halogen technology to produce infra-red light waves that heat up food quickly. Basically it's a glass container with a heating element built into the lid and fan that distributes heat quickly and evenly throughout the oven.

Generally the oven will come with a couple of removable cooking racks so that any fat produced simply drains away, making meat products healthier.

General Guidance

Cooking Times

All Halogen ovens will have their own variations when it comes to settings but that doesn't mean you can't use this guide.

For the sake of ease, I have based these instructions on my own oven which has settings of HI/MEDIUM/LOW. This equates to HI being approx 400F.

If you are at all unsure about which setting to use, by all means follow my instructions, but refer to your own user manual too, and I would suggest cooking for the least amount of time recommended and then checking whether the food is done.

Equipment needed

Obviously your oven will come with various pieces of equipment, but I would expect you to have the basic oven and then two grilling shelves. If you do not have these contact your manufacturer or the company you bought the oven from to purchase them. They make cooking vegetables and meat much easier.

I use the same equipment that I use with a normal oven and haven't had to buy anything special.

Helpful Cooking Tips

- Always check how well the food is cooked at minimum time.
- When baking multiple runs of foods, such as cookies, let the baking trays cool to room temperature between runs.
- Clean the oven interior and lamp covers frequently (after every use if possible).

Vegetables

Cooking vegetables at the same time as your meat can seem like a daunting task. It doesn't have to be, it just takes a bit more preparation. Vegetables will generally take longer to cook than the meat, so you will need to start cooking them first, particularly vegetables such as carrots and potatoes.

Potatoes

Your halogen oven is perfect for cooking all types of potatoes. I've found that baked potatoes are particularly good; nice and fluffy on the inside and crisp and brown on the outside.

- Baked Potatoes   44-46 minutes   Direct on rack
- Roast Potatoes   44-46 minutes   Direct on rack
- New Potatoes   44-46 minutes   In water in a dish
- Chips   20-22 minutes   Direct on rack

Carrots

Carrots will take about 25-27 minutes to cook in your Halogen Oven. I cook them in an ovenware or baking dish half filled with water. Or I place them directly on the rack to roast them.

Roasted Onion/Mushrooms

Roasted onions/mushrooms will take approximately 20-22 minutes. I generally place them directly on the grill; however I have had good results when I put them in a dish with some olive oil and seasoning.

Corn on the cob

Corn on the cob is delicious when cooked in a halogen oven and only take 10-12 minutes to cook. Remember to place the corn into a dish with a small amount of water in it or again simply grill it directly on the rack.

Recipes

Now that we've covered a few of the basics, we're going to try some of my family's favourites:

We'll start with how to cook a piece of meat with vegetables and then look at more complicated dishes and even how to cook Pasta, Bread and Desserts.

Buttered Roast Chicken, Roast Potatoes and Carrots

Ingredients
3lb chicken (45/48mins)
50g butter (room temperature)
6 King Edward potatoes
½ lb carrots
Salt and pepper to taste

Instructions

1. Remove the butter from the fridge and bring to room temperature

2. Cover the chicken with a light layer of butter and cover with foil

3. Peel and Chop carrots and peel and half potatoes

4. Place potatoes in an oven dish and carrots in oven dish and place into Halogen oven for 15 minutes on HI (400F).

5. After 15 minutes remove dish and check that carrots are beginning to soften. If they are still very hard leave in the oven for another 5 minutes.

6. Place chicken on lower metal grill inside the oven covered in foil and cook for 15 minutes, keeping a check on colour

7. After 15 minutes remove the foil and continue cooking for a further 15/18 minutes.

8. After 15/18 minutes pierce chicken with a skewer and check that the juices run clear.

9. Remove chicken and rest for 5 minutes before carving.

10. Remove vegetables and lightly season with salt and pepper.

11. Serve with chicken gravy.

BBQ Shrimp

Ingredients

3 lbs large shrimp, (about 45,
shelled, leaving the tails intact,
butterflied, and de-veined)
550ml spicy tomato base
barbecue sauce.

Directions

1. Insert a 10-inch bamboo skewer at the tail end of each
   shrimp and thread the shrimp onto it.

2. Brush the shrimp with the barbecue sauce and arrange
   them on the upper rack.

3. Just before grilling brush the shrimp again with the sauce,
   grill them on MEDIUM for 2~3 minutes on each side, or
   until they are pink and springy to the touch.

4. Serve them warm or at room temperature.

Chicken Nuggets

Ingredients
1 egg
275ml water
75g all-purpose flour
40g tempura mix
2 tsp salt & 1/4 tsp pepper
1 tsp onion powder
1/2 tsp seasoning or salt
1/8 tsp garlic powder
4 chicken breast fillet

Directions

1. Beat the egg and then combine it with 275ml water in a small, shallow bowl & stir

2. Combine the flour, salt, Accent, pepper, onion powder and garlic powder in a one zip lock/plastic food bag.

3. Pound each of the breast filets with a mallet until about 1/4-inch thick.

4. Trim each breast filet into bite sized pieces.

5. Coat each piece with the flour mixture by shaking in the bag.

6. Remove and dredge in the egg mixture, coating well. Then return each nugget to the flour/seasoning mixture.

7. Shake to coat. Put nuggets, bag and all, in the freezer for at least an hour.

8. Cover and refrigerate remaining egg mixture. After freezing, repeat the "coating" process.

9. Air fry the chicken Nuggets on halogen Oven on upper rack on HI for about 2 ~3 minutes per side (total 5 ~ 6 minutes) or until light brown and crispy.

Banana & Pumpkin Bread

Ingredients
1 450g box of cake mix (any variety)
2 eggs
3 bananas
450g Pumpkin
275ml milk
1 tsp cinnamon
1 tsp nutmeg
140g oil

Directions

1. Mash the bananas.
2. Add the slightly beaten eggs, milk, cinnamon, oil, and nutmeg and Mix well.
3. Add the cake mix half at a time making sure all mix is incorporated before adding the second batch.
4. Add 450g of pumpkin if wanting pumpkin bread.
5. Fill loaf tins 2/3 full.
6. Bake on full power/HI for 12 minutes uncovered.
7. The crust will form on top but it will not be done in the middle.
8. Put a little butter over the top and cover with tin foil allowing room for the bread to rise.
9. Bake for another 12 minutes on full power/HI.
10. The bread rises up in the middle.
11. The butter and tinfoil are essential for the last baking to prevent cracking.

BBQ Ribs

Ingredients
4 lbs pork spareribs
180g brown sugar
70ml ketchup
70ml soy sauce
70ml Worcestershire sauce
70ml rum
140ml chilli sauce
2 garlic clove, crushed
1 tsp
Brush top with mustard
1 dash ground black pepper

Directions

1. Cut spareribs into serving size portions, place on lower rack, and bake on HI for 6 minute per side.

2. In a bowl, mix together brown sugar, ketchup, soy sauce, Worcestershire sauce, rum, chilli sauce, garlic, mustard, and pepper.

3. Coat ribs with sauce and marinate at room temperature for 1 hour, or refrigerate overnight.

4. Place ribs on upper rack, and cook for 5~6 minutes per side.

Buttered lobster

Ingredients
2 lbs lobster
3 tbsp butter
1 dash salt and pepper
1 dash lemon juice

Directions

1. Remove lobster meat from shell and chop in cubes.

2. Melt butter.

3. In a shallow baking dish add lobster melted butter, lemon juice and salt & pepper.

4. Bake directly on rack for 10 to 12 minutes on HI (Full power)

5. Serve with lemon wedges.

Enchilada casserole

Ingredients
675g ground/minced beef
1 small onion
4 flour tortillas
300g olives
1 (300g) can refried bean
300g enchilada sauce
330g cheese

Directions

1. Place onion, meat and seasoning in dish and brown in Halogen Oven on HI (full power) for 2 mins or until brown. Drain grease.
2. Layer each tortilla with beans, meat, a spoonful of sauce, a couple of olives and cheese.
3. Roll tortillas and layer seam side down on dish.
4. Pour remaining sauce and olives on top. Bake 25-30 minutes.
5. Place remaining cheese on top for the last 2 minutes.

Garlic Mustard Chicken

Ingredients

1 chicken breast or pieces
3 large lemons, juice of 2
1 tbsp of Dijon mustard
2 tbsp garlic
1 tsp Cajun seasoning
1 tsp thyme
1 tsp sage
1 tsp rosemary

Directions

1. Combine all the above ingredients in a bowl and marinate the chicken breast in it for 1-3 hours.

2. Place on the lower oven rack on HI (full power) and cook until tender and juicy. (About 6-8 minutes per side).

Glazed grilled salmon

Ingredients
3 tbsp packed dark brown sugar
4 tsp prepared Chinese hot
mustard or Dijon mustard
1 tbsp soy sauce
1 tsp rice vinegar
2 (200g) salmon steaks (about
3/4-inch thick)

Directions

1. Combine brown sugar, mustard and soy sauce in medium bowl; whisk to blend.

2. Transfer 1 tablespoon glaze to small bowl; mix in rice vinegar and set aside.

3. Brush 1 side of salmon steaks generously with half of glaze in medium bowl.

4. Place salmon steaks, glazed side down, onto upper rack.

5. Grill for about 4 minutes on HI (full power).

6. Brush top side of salmon steaks with remaining glaze in medium bowl.

7. Turn salmon over and grill until second side is just opaque in centre, about 4 minutes.

8. Transfer salmon to plates.

9. Drizzle reserved glaze in small bowl over salmon and serve with chives.

Chicken and Jalapeño Quesadillas

Ingredients

4 tortillas
2 tbsp vegetable oil
340g Mexican cheese (shredded)
340g roasted deli chicken
(shredded)
60g fresh coriander (chopped)

Directions

1. Brush 2 tortillas with oil.

2. Place tortillas, oil side down, on small baking tray.

3. Sprinkle each with 1/4 of cheese, half of chicken, half of coriander, and 1/4 of cheese,

4. Top each with 1 tortilla, pressing to adhere; brush top with oil.

5. Bake quesadillas in Halogen Oven on HI (full power) until filling is heated through and edges begin to crisp, about 2~3 minutes.

6. Using large metal spatula, turn each over and bake until bottom is crisp, about 1~2 minutes.

7. Transfer quesadillas to plates. Cut into wedges and serve.

T Bone steaks

Ingredients

1 (2 1/2 lb) t bone steak (2-inch-thick)
1 tsp salt, plus additional for sprinkling (preferably sea salt)
1 tbsp olive oil, for drizzling

Directions

1. Pat steaks dry and rub all over with 1 teaspoon salt.

2. To cook steaks use upper grill and on HI, bake for about 9 minutes per side.

3. Transfer steaks to a cutting board and let stand, uncovered, 10 minutes.

4. Cut each section of meat off bone, then slice each piece crosswise against the grain and arrange slices on a platter.

5. Sprinkle lightly with salt and drizzle with oil.

Baked Swordfish with Olives

Ingredients

100g/150g swordfish steaks
(about 3/4 ins).
75g oil-cured green olives,
chopped pitted
75g oil-cured black olives,
chopped pitted
60g roasted red pepper chopped
1 tbsp parsley
2 anchovy fillet, minced
2 tsp caper, drained
1 tsp red wine vinegar
1 large garlic clove, minced
3 tbsp olive oil

Directions

1. Combine all olives, roasted peppers, parsley, minced anchovies, capers, vinegar and garlic in small bowl.

2. Stir in 1 tablespoon olive oil.

3. Season with salt and pepper.

4. Let stand 1 hour. (Can be made 1 day ahead. Cover and chill)

5. Place swordfish steaks on upper rack. Brush swordfish on both sides with remaining 2 tablespoons olive oil.

6. Season with salt and pepper.

7. Bake on HI (full power) just until fish is cooked through, about 5 minutes per side and then transfer to platter.

8. Spoon olive relish over swordfish and serve

Vegetable Lasagne

Ingredients
1 (300g) package fresh lasagne
(cooked)
2 egg, beaten
400g container ricotta cheese
300g cans condensed cream of
mushroom soup
450g cheddar cheese (shredded)
450g parmesan cheese (grated)
275ml sour cream
25g garlic and herb seasoning
250g package frozen broccoli,
thawed & chopped fine
250g package frozen carrots
(grated)

Directions

1. Grease a 9x13 inch lasagne dish.

2. In a medium bowl combine eggs, Ricotta cheese, mushroom soup, Cheddar cheese, Parmesan cheese, sour cream and soup mix.

3. In prepared dish layer lasagne sheets, cheese mixture, broccoli, carrots.

4. Repeat layers with remaining ingredients, ending with cheese.

5. Place in the oven covered with tinfoil, on HI (full power) for 15 minute

6. Uncover and cook an additional 15 minutes on HI.

Breaded Lemon Pepper Chicken with Roasted Asparagus

Ingredients
4 frozen boneless skinless
chicken breast
115g crushed cracker
crumb/bread crumbs
2 medium lemon
1 dash fresh ground pepper
1 dash salt
1 bunch fresh asparagus
1 tbsp oil

Directions

1. Clean & prepare your asparagus, place in a bowl and pour oil or melted butter on top, sprinkle with salt and toss, set aside.
2. Zest both lemons and mix the zest with the cracker/bread crumbs.
3. Place the frozen chicken breasts on a rack.
4. Squeeze one lemon half over the top of all the chicken breasts and sprinkle with salt.
5. Cover the top of each chicken breast with about a 1/4 inch layer of crumbs, press down.
6. Squeeze another lemon half over the crumbs then add freshly ground pepper (you can add as much or little as you like).
7. Heat on high for 15 minutes or until the crumbs begin to brown (add more time if necessary).
8. Turn chicken breasts over and repeat steps 3-7.
9. Add the asparagus to the bottom rack; replace the chicken on the rack over the asparagus.
10. Cook on HI for another 15 minutes or until the crumbs are browned and the asparagus is done.

Chocolate Chip & Walnut Cookies

Ingredients
175g all-purpose flour
40g unsweetened cocoa powder
1/2 tsp salt
450g chocolate chips, frozen
1hr
170g unsalted butter, diced,
room temperature
180g sugar
1 large egg yolk
2 tsp vanilla extract
3/4 tsp almond extract
225g walnut, coarsely chopped

Directions

1. Whisk flour, cocoa, and salt in small bowl to blend.
2. Coarsely chop 340g chocolate chips in processor.
3. With machine running, add butter, then half of sugar.
4. Add egg yolk and both extracts and process to blend.
5. Using on/off turns, mix in walnuts, scraping down sides of bowl occasionally.
6. Add flour mixture and process just until dough comes together, about 1 minute.
7. Transfer dough to large bowl and using hands, mix in remaining chocolate chips.
8. Using 1 tablespoon dough for each, shape dough into 1 1/4-inch-diameter balls.
9. Press each dough ball into ½ inch disc; dip 1 side into remaining sugar to coat.
10. Arrange cookies, sugar side up, on baking sheet (small). Bake cookies on HI until set and almost firm to touch, about 10 minutes; cool on racks.

Spicy Pork Chops and Baby Bok Choy

Ingredients
90g black bean garlic sauce
3 large garlic clove, minced
1 1/2 tbsp soy sauce
1 1/2 tbsp oriental sesame oil
1 tbsp fresh lime juice
1 tbsp finely chopped peeled
fresh ginger
4 boneless centre cut pork chop
(about 200g each)
4 baby bok choy, halved
lengthwise
2 tbsp chopped fresh coriander
4 lime wedge

Directions

1. Whisk together black bean sauce, garlic, soy sauce, sesame oil, lime juice, and ginger in shallow dish.

2. Set 2 tablespoons marinade aside.

3. Add pork to remaining marinade; let stand 20 minutes.

4. Remove pork from marinade; brush cut side of bok choy with reserved 2 tablespoons marinade.

5. Place pork on upper rack and cook on HI (full power) for about 8~10 minutes per side.

6. Grill bok choy until softened, about 8~10 minutes total.

7. Divide pork and bok choy among 4 plates.

8. Sprinkle with coriander, garnish with lime wedges, and serve.

Paprika lamb casserole

Serves 4

Ingredients

30g unsalted Butter
1 tbsp Olive oil
1kg diced Lamb, from the middle neck or shoulder, trimmed
of fat
1 large Onions, sliced
2 tsp plain flour
2 tsp Paprika
150ml brown stock
1 x 400g tinned chopped tomatoes
1 tsp caraway seeds
boiled Potatoes, to serve

Instructions

1. Heat oil and butter in a casserole dish. Add the lamb and brown on all sides over a high heat.

2. Take the meat out of the dish and leave on one side.

3. Add the onion to the same pan and soften for about 5 minutes over a low heat. Stir in the flour and paprika.

4. Pour in the stock and stir to mix before adding the tomatoes and caraway seeds.

5. Return the lamb to the dish and season with salt.

6. Cover the dish with foil and cook in the Halogen Oven on LOW for about 30 minutes or until the lamb is tender.

7. Remove any fat from top of the casserole, and serve with boiled potatoes.

Roasted Italian Potatoes

Ingredients
6 medium potatoes
Olive oil
Sea Salt
Parmesan cheese

Directions

1. Scrub but do not peel potatoes
2. Cut into 4 large chips/chunks.
3. Put potatoes in a bowl and add olive oil and salt to taste
4. Mix together then place on lower rack
5. Cook on HI (full power) for 25 minutes
6. Sprinkle with parmesan cheese and cook for 5 minutes more

Fish burger

Serves 2

Ingredients

455 g fresh tuna steaks, minced
1 carrot, grated
80 g onion, chopped
15 ml olive oil
25 g chopped fresh chives
15 ml mayonnaise
2 eggs
35 g breadcrumbs
freshly ground black pepper to taste
garlic salt to taste

Instructions

1. In a large bowl, mix together tuna, carrot, onion, chives, eggs, breadcrumbs, and mayonnaise.

2. Season with garlic salt and black pepper. Form into patties.

3. Arrange patties directly onto the Halogen Oven lower rack.

4. Cook, uncovered on HI for 10 minutes per side, or until golden brown.

Chorizo & Brandy Chicken

Ingredients
2 tbsp vegetable oil
4 chicken breasts
570ml/1 pint hot chicken stock
1 onion, peeled and quartered
2 cloves & few sprigs fresh thyme
1 carrot & 1 celery stick, halved
2 bay leaves & 4 garlic cloves
1 tsp smoked paprika
1 tbsp plain flour
1 tbsp unsalted butter
4 tbsp brandy
110g/4oz cured chorizo sausage
salt and black pepper
110g/4oz Manchego cheese

Directions

1. Bring the stock to the boil in a large saucepan. Stud one of the onion quarters with the two cloves and add to the pan along with the remaining onion, the chicken, carrot, celery, bay leaves, thyme, paprika and garlic. Cook for 20 minutes.

2. Place the chicken into a suitable sized tin or dish and strain the stock through a sieve into a bowl.

3. For the sauce, return the strained stock to a pan, bring to the boil and simmer until the liquid has reduced by half.

4. In a bowl, for the sauce, mash the flour and butter together to make a paste and then whisk along with the brandy and simmer for 3-4 minutes, until thickened and smooth.

5. Add the chorizo and season, to taste, with salt and freshly ground black pepper.

6. Pour this sauce over the chicken in the tin and sprinkle over the grated cheese.

7. Transfer to the oven and bake on HI (full power) for 18-20 minutes, or until the cheese is bubbling and lightly browned.

Spanish chicken casserole

Ingredients

3 tbsp olive oil
2 onions, sliced
8 skinless chicken thighs
1 tbsp plain flour, seasoned with a
little salt and pepper
290ml/½ pint chicken stock
Grated zest of 1 orange
Juice of 2 oranges
150ml/¼pt sherry
1 tbsp Worcestershire sauce
300g/10oz button mushrooms,
sliced
2 tbsp fresh parsley, chopped
Salt and pepper

Boiled rice, to serve

Directions

1. Cover the chicken in the seasoned flour.

2. Add 1 tbsp of oil & onions to the oven dish, and then add the chicken.

3. Add the chicken stock, onions and their juices, orange juice and zest, sherry and Worcestershire sauce.

4. Cover and cook for 18-20 minutes on HI (full power) until the chicken is tender.

5. Stir in the mushrooms and cook for approx 5 minutes.

6. Taste and season with salt and black pepper if necessary. Just before serving, sprinkle over the chopped parsley and serve with boiled rice.

Lime chicken

Ingredients

415ml fresh lime juice (12 limes)
3 garlic cloves, minced
2 teaspoons achiote paste
1 teaspoon dried oregano leaves
1 teaspoon ground cumin
1 1/2 lbs boneless skinless
chicken thighs, (1-inch pieces)
2 jalapeno chillies
1 (500g) jar guava shells in syrup
1 tablespoon coriander, chopped

Directions

1. Blend 275ml lime juice, garlic, achiote paste, oregano, and cumin in processor until smooth.

2. Season marinade to taste with salt and pepper.

3. Place marinade in medium bowl.

4. Add chicken; stir to coat.

5. Cover and refrigerate chicken overnight.

6. Place chillies on small baking sheet (on upper rack).

7. Roast on HI until soft, for about 10 minutes.

8. Stem and seed chillies and transfer to processor with pureed guava, reserved guava syrup, coriander, and remaining 140ml lime juice - Process until smooth.

9. Season sauce to taste with salt and pepper.

10. Transfer to medium bowl and cover and refrigerate but bring to room temperature before using

11. Remove chicken from marinade and divide among 8 eight-inch wooden skewers.

12. Grill on HI (full power) until chicken is cooked, turning once, 8 minutes each side.

Jerk Chicken

Ingredients
6 chicken breasts or 16 large
chicken wings
225g/8oz onions, quartered
2 habaneros or scotch bonnet
chillies, halved and seeded
50g/2oz fresh root ginger, peeled
and roughly chopped
½ tsp ground allspice
the leaves from 15g/½oz fresh
thyme sprigs
1 tsp freshly ground black pepper
120ml/4fl oz white wine vinegar
120ml/4fl oz dark soy sauce

Directions

1. Put all the ingredients for the jerk sauce into a food processor until smooth.

2. Place the chicken in a large shallow dish, pour over the sauce, cover and leave to marinate in the fridge for 24 hours, turning the chicken every now and then

3. Barbecue the chicken breasts or wings in oven for 10 minutes on HI (full power).

4. Baste with the leftover sauce.

5. Place back in oven for a further 10 minutes (or until done to your taste

6. As it cooks the thick sauce will go black in places, but as it falls off it will leave behind a really well flavoured, crisp skin, with lovely moist tender meat underneath.

Chicken Kiev

Ingredients

4 x 175g/6oz chicken breasts,
skin removed
3 garlic cloves, crushed
1 lemon, juice only
salt and black pepper
1 tbsp chopped fresh tarragon
300g/10½oz butter,
2 tbsp plain flour
1 free-range egg, beaten
10-12 tbsp fresh breadcrumbs
olive oil, for frying
250g/9oz cooked white rice
100g/3½oz bacon lardons, fried
1 tbsp chopped fresh parsley
100g/3½oz pine nuts, toasted
2 tbsp melted butter

Directions

1. For the chicken Kiev, slice into each chicken breast horizontally to make a pocket.

2. Place the garlic, lemon juice, salt and freshly ground black pepper, tarragon and butter into a bowl and mix well.

3. Stuff this mixture into the pocket in the chicken breasts and pull the flesh back over to enclose the filling.

4. Cover the chicken breasts in the flour, then dip into the beaten egg, then the breadcrumbs to coat completely, shaking off any excess.

5. Transfer to the oven and bake on HI (full power) for 18-20 minutes, or until golden-brown and completely cooked through (important to check this when stuffing chicken)

6. For the rice, place all the rice ingredients into a bowl

Chicken with Lemons and Olives

Ingredients

½ tsp saffron threads, crushed
250ml/9fl oz chicken stock
3 tbsp olive oil
3 onions, chopped
1 tsp ground ginger
1 tsp ground cumin
3 garlic cloves, finely sliced
1 free-range chicken (4lbs),jointed
1 tsp black peppercorns, crushed
6 small preserved lemons,
quartered, or 2 larger ones,
chopped (these are available from
many supermarkets)
100g/3½oz mixed olives
handful coriander leaves, chopped
handful flatleaf parsley, chopped

Directions

1. Warm the chicken stock in a saucepan and add the saffron threads to infuse.

2. Meanwhile, in a casserole dish or tin, heat the olive oil and fry the onions until soft.

3. Add the ginger, cumin and garlic and cook gently (LO – lowest setting) for a couple of minutes.

4. Add the chicken and stir to coat with the onion and spices.

5. Sprinkle in the crushed peppercorns and add the lemons and saffron-infused stock.

6. Place in oven and cook at HI (Full power) for about one hour, or until the chicken is falling apart.

7. Add the olives and leave for another ten minutes. Add the chopped coriander and parsley just before serving.

8. Serve with potatoes, crusty bread or rice and a green salad

Chicken with spiced plums

Ingredients
2kg/4½lb chicken
25g/1oz butter
1 large onion, finely chopped
115g/4oz raisins
225g/8oz firm plums, halved,
6 juniper berries, lightly crushed
1 tsp ground cinnamon
1 tsp ground ginger
pinch freshly grated nutmeg
runny honey
1 orange, juice only
300ml/11fl oz chicken stock
300ml/11fl oz red wine
few sprigs fresh rosemary
salt and ground black pepper

Directions
1. Brown the chicken all over in a non-stick frying pan. Set aside, but reserve the juices in the pan.
2. Heat the butter, onion and raisins in an ovenproof dish, and cook in on MEDIUM until softened.
3. Add the plums, juniper berries, cinnamon, ginger and nutmeg, and stir through. Drizzle in a little honey and pour in orange juice.
4. Pour in the chicken stock and red wine and then add a few sprigs of rosemary.
5. Season liberally with salt and freshly ground black pepper.
6. Add the chicken, place in the oven and cook on HI (full power) for about 1 hour, basting several times.
7. The plums will stew down and create a sauce to go with the chicken.
8. The chicken will be cooked when the juices from the thigh run clear when pierced with a skewer.

Balsamic and mozzarella chicken

Ingredients

1 skinless, boneless chicken breast
1 bottle balsamic vinaigrette salad dressing
1 small tomato, sliced
90 g fresh mozzarella cheese, sliced
1/8 bunch fresh basil leaves
3 ml balsamic vinegar
salt and freshly ground black pepper to taste

Instructions

1. Place chicken in a shallow dish or large resealable plastic bag. Pour the dressing over it, cover or seal, and marinate in the refrigerator for 12 to 24 hours.

2. Remove the chicken from the marinade and discard the marinade. Cook the chicken over low heat directly on the rack of your Halogen Oven for about 18-20 minutes, or until juices run clear.

3. Arrange chicken on a serving platter. Place a generous slice of fresh mozzarella on top of each piece.

4. Place a leaf of basil on top of the cheese, and cover with a slice of tomato. Dash balsamic vinegar over the platter, and season with salt and pepper.

Fillet of beef with stout

Ingredients
500g/1lb beef fillet, trimmed
150ml stout
150ml strong beef or veal stock
2 shallots, chopped
1 bay leaf
1 tsp brown sugar
25g/1oz butter
salt and pepper

Directions

1. Poach the whole piece of fillet in a mixture of the stout and stock with the chopped shallots and bay leaf for about 30 minutes on HI (the beef should be rare in the middle so keep an eye on it).

2. Remove the meat and keep warm.

3. Add the sugar to the stock mixture and reduce by about one third, finally adding the butter to make the sauce thick and shiny.

4. Season to taste with salt and pepper.

5. Pour the sauce on to white plates, then slice the beef thinly and arrange decoratively.

Lamb Roasted with Coffee

Ingredients
Cream or milk for serving
4 1/2 lb leg of lamb
Salt & freshly-ground black
pepper
Little butter or oil
Generous cup of coffee, medium
strength
2 tbs light cream
1 tsp sugar
2 Tbs flour 1 tsp red currant jelly

Directions
1. Mix together the coffee, light cream and sugar.

2. Rub meat with butter or oil and season well.

3. Place meat in roasting tin and roast at HI (full power) for 30 mins on the lower rack.

4. Then add the white, sweetened coffee to the pan and continue roasting for another 30 mins or until joint cooked to your liking, basting as before. When done, remove meat and keep warm.

5. Strain the pan juices then skim fat off the top and return 2 tablespoons to the roasting pan with the 2 tablespoons of flour.

6. Cook over a moderate heat for a few minutes, stirring all the time, then make a smooth sauce with the degreased juices and red currant jelly, made up with additional light cream or milk, scraping the bottom of the roasting pan well to incorporate any crusty bits with all their flavour.

7. Adjust seasoning, simmer 5-10 minutes then serve with the meat.

Sausage and Potato Bake

Ingredients
6 Thick Pork Sausages
500g frozen Southern style hash brown potatoes
450g shredded Cheddar Jack cheese combination
115g sliced green onions
115g diced green pepper
2 eggs, slightly beaten
275ml sour cream
½ tsp salt
¼ tsp. black pepper

Directions

1. Combine potatoes, chopped sausages, 330g cheese, green onions and pepper in large bowl. Mix well.

2. In small bowl, blend eggs, sour cream, salt and pepper.

3. Pour over potato mixture and blend well.

4. Spoon into buttered 9-inch square clear glass baking dish.

5. Place in oven and cover loosely with tin foil and cook on HI (full power) for 20-22 minutes

Pork Chops with Apple Mustard Glaze

Ingredients

4 boneless pork loin chops, cut
¾-inch thick (about 1 ¼ lb.)
Olive Oil
½ tsp. seasoned salt
¼ tsp. coarse black pepper
70ml country style Dijon mustard
45g firmly packed brown sugar
2 tbsp. honey
115g diced unpeeled apple

Directions

1. Brush top of each chop with oil.

2. Blend together the seasonings and sprinkle ½ over the chops.

3. Place chops on the rack in bake/broil pan for 5 minutes on HI (full power)

4. Turn chops over; brush with oil and add remaining seasoning mixture.

5. Return dish to oven for a further 5 minutes.

Parmesan Lobster Tail

Ingredients
340g cooked yellow rice
170g diced yellow squash
170g diced courgette
115g cup diced tomato
2 tbsp. olive oil
2 lobster tails, split lengthwise (
about 5 oz., ea.)
1 tbsp. melted butter
1 tbsp. fresh lemon juice
1 tbsp. grated Parmesan cheese

Directions

1. In medium bowl, combine rice, squash, courgettes, tomatoes and oil.

2. Spoon into greased shallow baking dish.

3. Arrange lobster tails; cut side up, on top of rice mixture.

4. Combine melted butter and lemon juice. Brush over lobster.

5. Sprinkle with Parmesan cheese.

6. Place baking dish inside oven for 20 minutes on HI (full power) checking regularly for when it is done.

7. Simply add a tossed salad and crisp dinner rolls.

Smoked Salmon & Onion Frittata

Ingredients

6 large eggs
275ml double cream
115g chopped green onions
1/2 tsp. salt
1/4 tsp. black pepper
275ml sour cream
1/2lb. thinly sliced smoked
salmon
2 tbsp. capers

Directions

1. In medium bowl, combine eggs, cream, green onions, salt and pepper.

2. Pour into buttered, 8-inch, clear glass baking dish.

3. Place directly on lower rack and cook on MEDIUM for 20 minutes. Check whether the mixture is now firm and if not cook for further 5 minutes.

4. Remove to cooling rack and cool for at least 30 minutes.

5. Spread sour cream over top to within 1/2-inch of edges.

6. Arrange smoked salmon on top.

7. Garnish with capers.

8. To serve, cut into 2-inch squares.

Goat's Cheese & Tomato Crostini

Ingredients
12 slices French bread, cut 3/4-inch thick
3 tbsp. olive oil
4 oz/100g goats cheese, at room temperature
2 tbsp. finely chopped sun-dried tomatoes, packed in oil
2 tbsp. chopped fresh basil
1/4 tsp. salt
1/8 tsp. black pepper
Basil leaves
Sun-dried tomatoes

Directions

1. Lightly brush both sides of slices of bread with olive oil.

2. Place directly on rack in Oven and cook for 5 minutes on MEDIUM.

3. Meanwhile, in medium bowl, blend goats cheese, sun-dried tomatoes, basil, salt and pepper until smooth and uniformly combined. (The mixture will become pink.)

4. Spread goats cheese mixture evenly over crostini.

5. Place back in oven and cook for 5 minutes on MEDIUM (or until golden brown)

6. Remove to serving tray and garnish with basil leaves and additional sun-dried tomatoes.

Banana Bread Pudding

Ingredients
900g cubed egg bread
1 ripe banana chopped
2 tbsp. minced candied ginger
1 tsp. dried orange peel
4 large eggs
825ml milk
205ml heavy cream
135g cup sugar
1 ½ tsp. vanilla extract
275ml heavy cream
2 tbsp. orange marmalade

Directions
1. Combine bread cubes, banana and ginger in 9-inch square clear glass baking dish.

2. In large bowl, combine eggs, milk, heavy cream, sugar and vanilla; blend well.

3. Pour mixture evenly over dish containing bread and banana.

4. Cook for 55 minutes on HI (full power) and cover with foil last 15 minutes of baking. (To test for doneness, insert a metal knife into the centre of the pudding; the knife should come out clean.)

5. Remove to cooling rack.

6. Meanwhile, combine heavy cream and marmalade in small deep bowl.

7. Serve pudding warm garnished with whipped cream.

Pear and Apple Crisp

Ingredients

450g fresh apple slices, cut in half
450g fresh pear slices, cut in half
1 tbsp. arrowroot
28g all-purpose flour
28g old-fashioned oats
180g firmly packed brown sugar
115g cold butter or margarine,
cubed
115g chopped almonds
1 tbsp. dried orange peel
½ tsp. ground cinnamon

Directions

1. In a clear glass baking dish, blend fruit and arrowroot.

2. In medium bowl, combine the flour, oats, brown sugar and butter.

3. Blend with fingers to form large crumbs.

4. Stir in almonds, orange peel and cinnamon.

5. Sprinkle evenly over fruit.

6. Cover baking dish with aluminium foil and cook for 30 minutes on HI (full power) removing foil for last 5 minutes.

7. Remove from oven and let stand on wire rack at least 30 minutes before serving.

8. Serve topped with vanilla ice cream or whipped cream.

Caribbean Scones

Ingredients
285g baking mix
45g cup sugar
60g butter or margarine
115g chopped toasted almonds
75g flaked coconut
1 large egg
70ml heavy cream
½ tsp. vanilla extract
1 can (205g) crushed pineapple,
well drained
Coarse sugar

Directions

1. In large bowl, combine baking mix, sugar and butter.
2. Using pastry blender or 2 knives, cut in butter until mixture is crumbly.
3. In small bowl, blend together egg, cream and vanilla.
4. Add to dry ingredients along with pineapple. Stir to blend.
5. Drop approx 1inch size portions of mixture onto lightly greased baking pan about 2 inches apart.
6. Sprinkle with coarse sugar.
7. Place baking pan in oven and bake for 20 minutes on MEDIUM but check near end to see whether done.
8. Cool on wire rack until ready to serve
9. Repeat with remaining dough.
10. Makes about 12 scones.

Pecan Pie

Ingredients
1 unbaked 9-inch pastry pie
3 large eggs
90g granulated sugar
90g light brown sugar
275ml light corn syrup
5 tbsp. melted butter or margarine
1 1/2 tsp. vanilla extract
1/8 tsp. salt
450g lightly toasted halves or
coarsely chopped pecans

Directions

1. Line pastry-filled pie plate with foil and add pie weights, uncooked rice or dry beans to hold down crust.

2. Place pie plate in Oven and cook for 3 minutes on MEDIUM.

3. Remove from oven and, using pot holders, carefully remove foil and weights from pastry shell.

4. Replace pie plate in oven and cook for a further 3 minutes on HI then remove pastry to cooling rack.

5. In large bowl, using wire whisk, combine eggs, sugars and corn syrup, add butter, vanilla and salt; blend well. Stir in pecans.

6. Pour into partially baked pie crust.

7. Place filled pie in oven and bake on HI (full power) for 8 minutes with a tent of foil over the mixture

8. Check pie to see how well done it is. The edges of the filling should be firm and the centre slightly quivery.

9. Remove to cooling rack and cool for at least 1½ hours.

10. Serve warm or at room temperature.

11. Add sweetened whipped cream or vanilla ice cream.

Pumpkin Pie

Ingredients
1 can (375g) pumpkin
2 large eggs
90g granulated sugar
90g firmly packed light brown
sugar
1 tsp. ground cinnamon
1 tsp. ground ginger
1/2 tsp. grated nutmeg
1/4 tsp. ground cloves
1/4 tsp. salt
415ml cups light cream
1 unbaked 9-inch pastry pie crust
in pie plate

Directions

1. In large bowl, combine all ingredients, except pie crust; blend.

2. Carefully spoon into pastry crust.

3. Place pie plate in oven and cook on HI (full power) for 35 minutes

4. May be served upon cooling or refrigerated overnight.

5. Serve warm or at room temperature.

6. Add sweetened whipped cream or vanilla ice cream

Halogen Ovens & Cooking for the Elderly

Cooking for the elderly

"Cooking food for the elderly can be a huge responsibility and a difficult balancing act. Not only do you have to provide nutritionally good food, but quite often you have to think about physical act of eating the food.

This guide and recipe book has been put together with elderly people in mind, it isn't meant to replace guidance given by your GP or a nutritionist but hopefully will give you some fresh idea's.

Halogen Ovens are ideal for cooking quick and easy meals, whether for one person or a family. Later on in this guide we will provide you with a few recipes for inspiration"

Maryanne x

Important Information

Here are afew important things to remember:

1. Control portion sizes. People need fewer calories as they get older, and they should eat a balanced, moderate diet to keep their weight under control.

2. Read the information that comes with all medications to find out if there are any dietary restrictions that accompany the medication.

3. Try to lower the sodium (salt) intake of a senior citizen, especially if he or she is at risk for high blood pressure.

4. Make sure there is lots of fibre in the food you serve; this helps prevent constipation.

5. Serve low-sugar foods if the person you are feeding has diabetes or is at risk of becoming diabetic.

6. Serve heart-healthy foods ' low-fat, low-salt and preferably prepared from scratch. Prepare lots of whole grains and vegetables, and cut down on red meat.

7. Make sure there is lots of calcium in the food you are cooking, or offer an easily absorbed calcium supplement; this helps prevent bone loss and osteoporosis in older people, especially women.

8. Consult a hospital nutritionist or dietician if an older person needs to be hospitalized for any serious; this will prepare you for any dietary restrictions or nutritional requirements that you may not have considered.

9. Serve food that is easy on dentures, if necessary. Some foods are too chewy or too sticky for denture wearers to eat comfortably.

10. Monitor alcohol consumption; although the occasional glass of wine with dinner probably can't hurt, and may even benefit the heart to some degree, it's not a good idea for people of any age to drink too much, especially if medications are involved.

Tips & Warnings

This guide isn't meant to replace the advice given by professionals and it's important to remember the following:

1. One of the by-products of aging is often a gradual loss of the senses of taste and smell ' food may begin to seem bland. Try to spice it up with seasonings that don't contain salt and won't irritate sensitive stomachs.

2. Always ask the people you are feeding for suggestions, comments and special requests. They will almost certainly have specific tastes, likes and dislikes that you need to know about.

3. Encourage older people to stay active; a healthy diet is great, but regular exercise is important, too.

4. If you are concerned about the diet of an older person who lives alone, try to take a look inside the cupboards and fridge when you visit. Sometimes, especially after the loss of a spouse, seniors neglect themselves physically, and this can lead to malnutrition.

5. If your parent or loved one is taking a lot of over-the-counter remedies for indigestion or heartburn, encourage him or her to see a doctor. Sometimes these complaints can signal more serious health problems.

Recipes

Easy Chicken Casserole

(Serves 1)

Ingredients

1 Chicken stock cube

1 Chicken breast

Small tin of cream of mushroom soup

Dried Onion flakes

Instructions

1. Dissolve a chicken stock cube in 140g of hot water.

2. Reserve and refrigerate ½ of this to use later.

3. Measure 112g cup brown rice in an individual-size, oven-proof dish.

4. Pour the ½ of chicken stock over the rice.

5. Sprinkle with dehydrated onion flakes.

6. Top with 1 piece of uncooked chicken (breast or thigh works well).

7. Top with 1 tin cream of mushroom soup. Cover with aluminium foil.

8. Bake for 18-20 minutes on HI or full power.

9. Remove foil and continue baking for 5 mins or until chicken is browned. Serve with 1 slice of toasted whole wheat bread.

Special Chicken

(Serves 2)

Ingredients

1 whole chicken breast
1 can stewed tomatoes
1 green pepper, cut into chunks
1 medium onion, cut into chunks
1 clove garlic, minced
¼ tsp. curry powder
1 bay leaf
275ml chicken stock

Instructions

1. Simmer chicken breast in 450ml of water with bay leaf for 20 minutes. Remove and cool in refrigerator. Skim the fat from top of the stock when it is solidified.

2. Bone the chicken and combine with the chicken stock, stewed tomatoes, green pepper, onions, garlic and curry powder. Simmer for 20 minutes.

3. Thicken slightly with cornstarch and water.

4. Serve with rice, three-quarters of a cup per person. (Suggestion: Prepare the rice using leftover chicken stock.)

Cheese & Potato Pie

Ingredients

2 large baking potatoes (or equivalent quantity of smaller ones),
they need to be the floury sort
1 large white onion
2 large eggs
8 oz mature cheddar grated
Salt and pepper

Instructions

1. Parboil the potatoes in their skins, until just starting to soften.
2. Drain and allow to cool.
3. Finely slice or chop the onion.
4. When the potatoes are cool enough to handle, thickly slice them (1/4") and place one layer (say one third of the quantity) in a greased baking dish.
5. Season with salt and pepper.
6. Add one third of the chopped onion and one third of the grated cheese. Repeat the layers of seasoned potato, onion and cheese until all the ingredients are used up.
7. Beat up the eggs, pour over the potato layers and bake in oven on HI (full power) for about 40-45 minutes or until golden brown.

Tips

- Great served with sweetcorn and petit pois.

Steak hotpot

Ingredients

Oxo Cube
Potatoes
Tin of stewing steak
Cornflour
Carrots
Onions

Instructions

1. Place an oxo cube with potato cubes/slices and carrots and bake in Halogen Oven for approx 45 minutes or until potato is cooked.
2. Pour in a tin of stewing steak and add corn flour mixed with water to thicken to taste and cook for a further 5-10 minutes or until cooked through.

Tips

- You could do the same with a chicken oxo and tin of chicken supreme or similar.

Chicken & Mango Bake
(Serves 2)

Ingredients

2 chicken breasts/ thighs
2 small pots sour cream
Jar of Mango Chutney
Chopped Onions
Chopped mushrooms

Instructions

1. Add chicken breast, or thighs to a casserole dish, and cover with 2 pots of sour cream and 1 jar of Mango chutney.
2. Place in oven for 18 – 20 minutes on full power (HI) or until the chicken is cooked (Check that the juices run clear)
3. Add chopped onions or chopped mushrooms near the end and cook for a further 2-3 minutes.

Cheese Bubble and Squeak
(Serves 4)

Ingredients

675g (1.5lbs) Old potatoes, peeled and chopped
70ml Semi-skimmed milk
450g (2lbs) Green cabbage
2 Small onions, finely chopped
Black pepper to taste
90g (6oz) mature cheddar cheese, grated

Instructions

1. Boil the potatoes in water for approximately 20 minutes or until tender.
2. Drain the potatoes and cream with the milk.
3. Cook the cabbage for 5 minutes in water.
4. Chop the cabbage and add to the potato with the chopped onion.
5. Season to taste.
6. Spoon into a baking dish and top with the grated cheese.
7. Cook for 30 minutes on full power covered will aluminium foil.
8. Remove foil and cook for a further 5 minutes or until all ingredients soft.

Tips

- Why not spoon the ingredients into individual single serving baking dishes and freeze for future use.

Tasty Corned Beef Hash
(Serves 4)

Ingredients

450g (1lbs) Old potatoes, peeled
1 Onion, peeled and chopped
1 Green pepper, de-seeded and chopped
2 tbsp Sunflower or rapeseed oil
1 tsp Worcestershire sauce
340g Tinned corned beef, roughly chopped
Black pepper to taste

Instructions

1. Cook the potatoes in water in the Halogen oven for approximately 15 minutes or until tender (on full power or HI).
2. Drain and roughly chop the potatoes and add the onion and pepper.
3. Put these ingredients into an oven dish and add the Worcestershire sauce and corned beef.
4. Cook on a low heat for 5-10 minutes, stirring occasionally, until heated through.
5. Season and serve.

Cottage Pie
(Serves 6)

Ingredients

2 tbsp Sunflower or olive oil
1 Onions, chopped
675g (1.5 lb) Minced beef
3 tbsp Tomato puree
½ tbsp Worcestershire sauce
450ml Beef stock
1 kg Potatoes
60 ml Semi-skimmed milk

Instructions

1. Heat the oil in a pan and cook the onion and minced beef until evenly browned.
2. Mix in the tomato puree, Worcestershire sauce, beef stock and seasoning and bring to the boil.
3. Simmer gently for 20 minutes.
4. While doing the above, cook the potatoes in water in your Halogen oven for approximately 15 minutes or until tender.
5. Drain the potatoes and cream with the milk.
6. Place the meat mixture in an ovenproof dish and cover with the mashed potato.
7. Bake on full power for 10 minutes or until the top is golden. Serve immediately.

Tips

When recipes serve more than one, the best idea is to freeze any extra. If you use individual portions they can be re heated when needed.

Meat and Vegetable Stew
(Serves 6)

Ingredients

280 g Stewing Beef
1 tbsp Plain flour
½ tbsp Vegetable oil
250ml Water
2 large Onions, quartered
225 g Swede
112 g Parsnip
2 Carrots
2 tbsp Dried herbs
Freshly ground pepper to taste

Instructions

1. Cut all of the visible fat from the beef and discard.
2. Cut the beef into about 2.5cm (1 inch) cubes before coating it in flour until it is all used.
3. In a heavy pan, heat the oil over a medium-high heat. Add the beef and cook, stirring until brown on all sides.
4. In an oven dish add the water, onions, dried herbs and pepper.
5. Peel the swede, parsnips and carrots and cut into 2cm (0.75 inch) pieces.
6. Then add the swede, parsnips and carrots to the pan and cook on medium heat for 25 minutes or until the vegetables are tender.
7. Add the meat to this oven dish and cook on a medium heat for a further 10 minutes or until mixture is tender. Add extra pepper to taste.

Tips

- Use leaner cuts of meat such as flank and sirloin, if available.
- Cook meat without adding extra fat e.g. grill, roast or microwave or pour off the excess fat before adding the other ingredients. Alternatively, if you cook the stew a day in advance and refrigerate overnight the hardened fat from the surface could be removed before reheating.
- Additional vegetables could be added to increase the bulk.

Pear Crumble
(Serves 2)

Ingredients

20g margarine
25g Wholemeal flour
25g Porridge oats
15g Sugar
1 tsp Olive oil
300g Tinned pears in natural juice

Instructions

1. Make the crumble by rubbing the margarine into the flour and oats.
2. Stir in the sugar and oil.
3. Drain the pears.
4. Arrange half the pears in a baking dish.
5. Cover with half the crumble mixture.
6. Repeat steps 4 and 5 with the remaining pears and crumble mixture.
7. Bake in the oven on full power (HI) for 25 minutes (covered with foil) and remove foil for last 5 minutes
8. Cook for a further 5 minutes or until the top is golden brown.
9. Serve with either chocolate or custard sauce.

Eve's Pudding
(Serves 10)

Ingredients

900g (2 lb) Cooking apples
120g (4 oz) Demerara sugar
Finely grated rind of 2 lemons
240g (4 oz) Self-raising flour
180g (6 oz) Caster sugar
180g (6 oz) Sunflower margarine
4 Eggs, beaten

Instructions

1. Peel, core and slice the apples and place in an ovenproof dish in layers, sprinkling each with Demerara sugar and lemon rind.
2. Cream margarine and caster sugar together until light and fluffy.
3. Beat the eggs into the creamed mixture a little at a time, adding a little flour to prevent curdling.
4. Fold in the rest of the flour.
5. Spread the mixture over the fruit and bake for 25- 30 minutes on full power. Covered with foil. (To test for doneness, insert a metal knife/skewer into the centre of the pudding; the knife should come out clean.)
6. Remove foil for last 5 minutes of cooking
7. Serve with custard, yoghurt or fromage frais.

Rice Pudding
(serves 8)

Ingredients

100g (4oz) Short grain rice
1200ml (2 pints) Semi-skimmed milk
25g (1oz) Caster sugar
50g (2oz) Dried fruit, like sultanas or raisins
Few drops of vanilla essence or sprinkle of ground nutmeg or cinnamon

Instructions

1. Wash and drain the rice then place in a greased ovenproof dish.
2. Add the sugar, dried fruit and vanilla essence.
3. Pour in the milk and sprinkle with ground nutmeg or cinnamon, if desired.
4. Mix together and bake in the oven on a medium heat for 45 minutes or until a sticky consistency is achieved.
5. Serve hot or cold.

Tips

- Try using an artificial sweetener in place of the castor sugar.
- For a change, try tapioca, sago, barley, semolina or macaroni instead of rice.
- Try serving the rice pudding topped with different fruits e.g., orange segments, banana slices, or tinned peach or pear slices (drained of juice).

Stewed Fruit and Custard
(serves 8)

Ingredients

For the stewed fruit:
8 Cooking apples/pears
200g (8 oz) Raisins or currants
1 tbsp Water
50g (2oz) Caster sugar
Pinch of cinnamon
For the Custard:
1200ml (2 pints) Semi-skimmed milk
100g (4oz) Caster sugar
50g (2oz) Custard powder
Few drops of vanilla essence

Instructions

1. Peel, core and slice the apples or pears.
2. Put into the medium oven dish with the water, sugar, cinnamon, raisins or currants and cook on a low heat until the fruit becomes soft.
3. Mix the custard powder with a little milk.
4. Heat the remaining milk and before it reaches boiling point, stir in the custard paste.
5. Simmer until the custard thickens, stirring all the time.
6. Cook for a further 3 minutes, remove from the heat and stir in the sugar and vanilla essence before pouring over the fruit.
7. Serve hot.

Tips

- Save time and money by using tinned fruit in natural juices in place of the fresh fruit.
- Try using an artificial sweetener in place of the castor sugar to reduce the sugar content of the dish.
- Use ready made custard in a tin or carton

Baked Apples
(Serves 1)

Ingredients

1 Cooking apple
Sprinkling raisins
1 dessertspoon of Clear honey

Instructions

1. Wash and core the apple.
2. Score a line round apple, about a third of the way down from the top.
3. Place the apple in an ovenproof dish with 1 tablespoon of water.
4. Fill the empty core of apple with raisins and top off with honey.
5. Bake in the Halogen Oven for 25-30 minutes or until the apples are soft.
6. Serve with custard, yoghurt, or Fromage Frais.

Spiced lamb shanks

Ingredients

1 tbsp olive oil

8 small neatly trimmed lamb shanks

1 red onion, chopped

2 cloves garlic, sliced

1 tbsp grated ginger

1 tsp paprika

1 tsp turmeric

1 tsp ground cumin

1 tsp cardamom pods, bruised

1 cinnamon stick

2 tbsp brown sugar

4 large ripe tomatoes seeded, roughly chopped

4 cups chicken stock or water

2 potatoes, scrubbed and chopped (skin on)

1 sweet potato, peeled and chopped

Instructions

1. Heat oil in a large frying pan over a high heat.
2. Add lamb shanks and cook for 2 minutes on each side or until they are well browned. Remove lamb and place in a baking dish.
3. Reduce heat to medium and add onion to the pan. Cook for 5 minutes, stirring occasionally, until onion is soft.
4. Add garlic and ginger and cook for 1 minute longer, then add remaining spices. Cook for 2 minutes, stirring constantly.
5. Add sugar, tomatoes and stock and bring to the boil. Remove from heat.
6. Add potatoes and sweet potato to the baking dish with the lamb and pour the sauce over the top. Cover with foil and bake on a medium heat for 30-35 mins, or until the lamb falls away from the bone.
7. Serve with steamed couscous, a dollop of yoghurt and fresh coriander

Oven-baked fish with tomato and parsley

Ingredients

1 tbsp olive oil

1 onion, finely chopped

1/4 cup chopped flat-leaf parsley

2 garlic cloves, very thinly sliced

2 x 400g tins chopped tomatoes

Sea salt and freshly ground black pepper

4 x firm white fish fillets (such as blue eye, ling, snapper)

To serve

Mashed potato

Butter lettuce salad

Instructions

1. Heat the olive oil in a large ovenproof dish with a lid over a medium heat.

2. Add the onion and parsley, stirring occasionally for 5 minutes or until onion is soft. Add garlic and continue stirring for 1 minute.

3. Add the tomatoes, bring to the boil then reduce the heat to low and simmer for 10 minutes. Season, and then remove from heat.

4. Add the fish pieces to the dish, pushing the fish into the tomato mixture. Cover dish with aluminium foil and place in Halogen Oven for 10 minutes.

5. Remove foil from dish and return to oven for a further 5 minutes.

6. Serve fish with mashed potato and a butter lettuce salad.

Beef and Vegetable Casserole

Ingredients

500g (1lb 2oz) stewing beef cut into 1cm (½") pieces
500g (1lb 2oz) mixed onions, carrots, courgettes, red and green peppers and celery cut into 2.5cm (1") pieces
1 clove of garlic, crushed
1 tbsp tomato puree
1 tin chopped tomatoes
salt and pepper
25g (1oz) oil
25g (1oz) flour
500ml (1pt) stock or water

Instructions

1. Heat the oil and seal the beef and vegetables in a suitable pan.

2. Add garlic, tomato puree, salt and pepper.

3. Sprinkle over flour and continue cooking for 2 minutes.

4. Add tin of tomatoes and stock, heat until simmering then pour into the oven dish.

5. Place in Halogen oven and cook for 15 to 20 minutes on HI (full power), stirring occasionally from sides of pan, until the meat is tender.

Delicious Potato & Frankfurter Goulash

Ingredients

500g (1lb 2oz) potatoes, peeled and diced
200g (7oz) Frankfurters, cut in to 2cm (¾") pieces
1 large onion, finely chopped
2 cloves garlic, crushed
4 tsp sweet paprika
1 tsp dried marjoram
2 tsp caraway seed (optional)
salt and freshly ground black pepper
oil for cooking
1 tbsp flour (approx.)
1 tbsp crème fraîche

Instructions

1. Cook the onion in a saucepan until pale golden, add the garlic, paprika and the caraway seeds (if using).

2. Add to oven dish with potatoes, salt, a good cupful of water, cover and cook for 40 minutes on HI or until the potatoes are almost cooked.

3. Add the chopped Frankfurters, pepper, marjoram and sprinkle with a little of the flour to thicken the gravy; cook for a few minutes to heat through.

4. Finally let cool a little and stir in the crème fraîche

Sausage and Leek Hotpot

Ingredients

1 tbsp olive oil
350g (12oz) finely sliced leeks
6 plump Cumberland sausages
2 tablespoons plain flour
700g/1½lb potatoes, peeled and thinly sliced
30g (1½oz) butter, melted
200ml (6fl oz) vegetable stock (from a cube)
100g (4oz) mature Cheddar or Gruyère, grated (optional)
Salt and freshly ground black pepper

Instructions

1. Place the oil in the oven dish, add the sliced leeks, stir well to coat and cook for 15-20 minutes, stirring very occasionally.

2. In the meantime cut each sausage into three pieces and toss in the flour to lightly coat.

3. Melt the butter in a deep bowl, and coat and lightly season the sliced potatoes, stirring them well.

4. When the leeks have softened, add the sausage pieces and cover with the sliced potatoes.

5. Pour on the stock and cook on full power for about 45 minutes to 1 hour or until the potatoes are crispy and light brown.

6. Sprinkle on the grated cheese if desired and gently stir it into the pot and serve.

7. A tomato salad is a good accompaniment.

Fish with Cheese Sauce

Ingredients

15g (½oz) butter
225g (8oz) fillet of haddock or cod
Squeeze of lemon juice
Salt and freshly ground black pepper
1 packet Béchamel sauce mix
1 tbsp double cream
5 seedless green grapes cut in half
2 tbsp grated cheese

Instructions

1. Melt the butter and brush the base of the oven dish.

2. Brush the fish with the rest of the butter, place in the oven, squeeze the lemon over the fish and season lightly. Cook on a medium heat for 10 minutes.

3. Make the sauce according to the instruction on the packet. This will probably take you about 10 minutes by which time the fish will be almost cooked.

4. Add the cream and the grapes to the sauce and pour over the fish. Sprinkle with the grated cheese and cook for a further 4/5 minutes.

Baked Bananas

Ingredients

3 bananas cut in chunks
25g (1oz) butter
50g (2oz) soft brown sugar
1 lemon, grated rind and juice
1 orange, grated rind and juice
2-3 tbsp rum (optional)

Instructions

1. Arrange the banana pieces in the oven dish and dot with the butter
2. Sprinkle with the sugar and lemon and orange rind.
3. Mix together the fruit juices (and rum if using) and pour over the bananas.
4. Cover with foil and cook for 15 minutes or until piping hot. Serve hot with ice cream.

Plum toast

Ingredients

1 large thick slice of white bread, (preferably a day old), buttered on both sides
2 large plums,

2 rounded tbsp caster sugar

Instructions

1. Place the buttered bread in an oven dish.

2. Sprinkle with one tablespoon of sugar.

3. Cut each plum in half, remove the stone and place the four halves cut side down on the bread.

4. Brush the plums **very** lightly with water and sprinkle with the rest of the sugar. Cook for approx. 30 minutes on a medium heat. The bread should be crisp, the plums soft.

5. Serve with custard.

Tip

You can also use all different types of fruit including but not limited to bananas, apricots, peaches or orange.

Vegetarian Recipes for Halogen Ovens

Vegetarian Recipes for Halogen Ovens

"This recipe book has been put together for people who are vegetarian and are looking to use their Halogen Ovens.

Buts it important to remember a few things:

- *Eat a dark green vegetable (broccoli, spinach, kale, collard greens) at least three times a week. These nutritional powerhouses are packed full of vitamins such as calcium and iron. On the run or hate spinach? Try drinking your greens.*
- *Take a vitamin supplement that contains B12 or include nutritional yeast in your diet regularly, especially if you're vegan or mostly vegan.*
- *Water water water! It's been said over and over again for a reason- because its true! Most people don't drink nearly enough. Bring a water bottle with you wherever you go and invest in a simple filter for your home. Water is especially important when adjusting to a new way of eating, as it will help curb any cravings you may experience.*
- *Make it a goal to eat at least one piece of raw fruit or a handful of raw vegetables every day. Reduce your refined sugar intake. Keep your favourite salad dressings on hand. A little variety is great too— try to keep at least two kinds, either store bought or homemade on hand at all times.*
- *Eat the rainbow! Fruits and vegetables all contain different nutrients. A simple way to remember to eat a range of vitamins and minerals is to vary the colours of the vegetables you eat.*

Halogen Ovens are ideal for cooking quick and easy meals, whether for one person or a family."

Maryanne x

Stuffed peppers with pine nuts and couscous

Serves: 4

Ingredients

225g couscous, using vegetable stock instead of water

1/2 red onion

1 tablespoon olive oil

2 tomatoes, cut into wedges

100g sliced mushrooms

1 tablespoon pine nuts

80ml white wine

handful of chopped fresh herbs

2 large peppers, halved & de-seeded

Instructions

1. Prepare the couscous according to the packet instructions.
2. Fry the onion in olive oil. Add the tomatoes, mushrooms & pine nuts.
3. Pour in the wine, a good handful of chopped fresh herbs & season and continue to heat.
4. Sprinkle over couscous.
5. Stuff 4 large halves of pepper with the mixture & bake for 10 minutes on HI (Full power).

Soya Bolognaise

Serves 4

Ingredients

1 tablespoon vegetable oil

1 onion, chopped

2 cloves garlic, crushed

175g mushrooms, sliced

1 green pepper, chopped

350g Quorn mince

300ml vegetable stock, made up using 1 vegetable stock cube

1 x 400g can chopped tomatoes

3 tablespoons tomato puree

1 tablespoon mixed dried herbs

freshly ground black pepper

Instructions

1. Heat the oil in a large frying pan & fry the onion & garlic for 2 minutes.
2. Add the mushrooms & pepper & cook for 1 minute. Add the mince & cook for a further 2 minutes.
3. Add the stock, tomatoes, tomato puree, herbs & season well.
4. Cook for 10-15 minutes.
5. Serve with spaghetti & garnish with sage & rosemary.

Chickpea burger

Serves 4

Ingredients

1 x 420g can of chickpeas, drained & rinsed

120g hazelnuts, chopped

1 onion, finely chopped

2 carrots, grated

2 tablespoons sun-dried tomato puree

1 large egg, beaten

dried breadcrumbs for coating

freshly ground black pepper

To serve:

4 soft baps

crisp lettuce leaves

tomato ketchup, mayonnaise or tzatsiki

Instructions

1. In a large bowl, mash the drained chickpeas with a potato masher, or if you haven't a masher, clench your fist & pummel the chickpeas with your hand.
2. Stir in the hazelnuts, onions, carrots, tomato purée & egg & mix well. Season to taste.
3. Divide the mixture into 4 & shape into 4 flat burgers.
4. Coat the outside of each burger with the breadcrumbs and place in the fridge for 1 hour.
5. Grill the burgers on the lower grill for 2 minutes on each side, turning carefully.
6. Serve the chickpea burgers in the soft baps with accompaniments

Jacket potato with sour cream filling

Serves 4

Ingredients

4 large potatoes

284ml carton soured cream

½ teaspoon chilli powder

3 tablespoons snipped chives

1 tablespoon chopped dill

2 tablespoons capers

chive sprigs to garnish

freshly ground black pepper

Instructions

1. Mix together the filling ingredients in a bowl, cover with cling film & chill until required.
2. Prick the potatoes & brush with oil.
3. Place in halogen oven directly onto the grill for 45/50 minutes (on full power), until cooked to taste
4. Remove half of the potato and mix with filling.
5. Serve with a spoonful of filling, garnished to taste

Potato with Mozzarella

Serves 4

Ingredients

750g bag baby new potatoes

3 cloves garlic, peeled and chopped

2 x 125g packs low fat Mozzarella, drained & diced

few sprays one calorie oil

freshly ground black pepper

1 red & 1 yellow pepper, deseeded & chopped

4 ripe tomatoes, chopped

20g pack fresh basil, torn

Instructions

1. Place the potatoes & peppers in a roasting tin & toss with the garlic, oil & seasoning.
2. Place in the oven for 40 minutes, then stir in the tomatoes & sprinkle over the mozzarella.
3. Cook for a further 5 minutes or until the mozzarella is melted.

Soft Blue Cheese Pasta Bake

Serves 4

Ingredients

250g dried egg pasta shapes

2 tablespoons olive oil

1 clove garlic, crushed

1 red pepper, deseeded & diced

1 bunch salad onions, sliced

125g button mushrooms, quartered

50g mange tout, diamond cut

175g soft blue cheese (i.e. dolcelatte), roughly crumbled

1 tablespoon freshly chopped parsley

1 medium size egg, beaten

4 tablespoons single cream

75g half-fat mozzarella cheese, grated

Instructions

1. Cook the pasta following the pack instructions.
2. Meanwhile, heat the oil in a large saucepan & cook the garlic, onion, mushrooms, pepper & mange tout, until softened.
3. Stir in the crumbled cheese, cream, parsley & seasoning, to taste. Then add the egg & the drained pasta.
4. Spoon into a lightly greased ovenproof dish & sprinkle with the mozzarella cheese.
5. Place in the oven for 10 minutes on HI (full power) or until golden brown & bubbling

Cheese & Onion Bread Bake

Ingredients

1tbsp corn oil
1 large onion, finely chopped
½tsp thyme
4½oz / 125g reduced-fat Cheddar cheese, grated
3oz/75g parmesan cheese, grated
1dsp freshly chopped chives
8 medium slices of wholemeal bread, crusts removed
3 medium free-range eggs
18floz/500ml skimmed milk
black pepper

Instructions

1. Brush a baking dish with a little oil.
2. Heat the remaining oil in a frying pan and fry the onions with the thyme over a gentle heat, stirring occasionally, for 15-20 minutes until very soft and just turning golden.
3. Mix the cheeses and the chives in a small bowl.
4. Put 4 slices of bread on the bottom of the prepared dish ensuring that they fit exactly.
5. Cover with the onion mixture and half the cheese mixture. Put the other slices of bread over and cover with the remaining cheese.
6. Whisk the eggs and milk together in a bowl and season with pepper.
    Pour this over the bread and cheese mixture.
7. Bake for 15 minutes, or until puffed up and golden

Vegetable & Nut Roast
Serve 4

Ingredients

1 carrot, scraped
1 onion, peeled
1 stick celery
200g mixed nuts (e.g. almonds, peanuts, brazil nuts)
2tsp Marmite
2 free range eggs
1 or 2 tsp mixed herbs
salt & pepper
Dried breadcrumbs (for coating tin)

Method

1. Put all the ingredients into a food processor and process until vegetables and nuts are chopped into chunky pieces.
2. Put into a bowl and mix with remaining ingredients.
3. Line a suitable sized loaf tin with a strip of non-stick paper, grease well and sprinkle with dry breadcrumbs.
4. Spoon mixture into tin and level the top.
5. Bake covered with foil for 20 minutes and then uncovered for the last 10 minutes until set.

Baked Mushrooms filled with Spinach, Brie and Walnuts

Serves 4

Ingredients:
4 field or portabello mushrooms, wiped and stalks removed
45ml/3tbsp olive oil
100g/4oz vegetarian Brie cut into small chunks
225g/8oz baby leaf spinach
40g/1 ½ oz walnuts, chopped
to taste salt and black pepper

Instructions

1. Heat the oil in a frying pan and fry the mushrooms on both sides until tender. Remove and place in a greased ovenproof dish in a single layer.
2. Wash the spinach and cook quickly in the frying pan until wilted. Drain well and use to top each of the mushrooms.
3. Mix the walnuts and Brie together in a bowl and season well.
4. Cover the mushrooms with the mixture and place in oven for 5 minutes and cook until the cheese is bubbling and golden. (may take longer than 5 minutes on HI)

Aubergine and Halloumi Rolls
Serves 4

Ingredients
1 large aubergine
225g/8oz halloumi, cut into 8 pieces
150ml/1/4 pint olive oil
salt for sprinkling
40ml/8tsp sundried tomato paste
16 cocktail sticks, soaked in water for 30 minutes
8 basil leaves

Instructions

1. Trim the end and slice the aubergine into 8 thin slices, lengthways. Place on a baking tray and sprinkle with salt.
2. Leave for 30-60 minutes until the bitter juices have been extracted and the slices are pliable. Rinse well and pat dry on kitchen towel.
3. Season the olive oil with freshly ground black pepper and brush over one side of each slice.
4. Spread 1 teaspoon of sundried tomato paste over each slice then place a basil leaf topped with a piece of halloumi on one end and roll up.
5. Secure by skewering with two criss-crossed cocktail sticks.
6. Brush the outside of the rolls with olive oil and cook on HI for about 4-5 minutes on each side until tender.

Beef Tomatoes with Marinade

Serves 4

Ingredients

4 ripe beef tomatoes
20ml/4tsp balsamic vinegar
freshly ground black pepper
30ml/2tbsp olive oil
10g/¼ oz fresh basil leaves
8 olives to garnish

Instructions

1. Cut the tomatoes in half, and then make shallow criss-cross cuts over each cut side. Drizzle a little balsamic vinegar over each and season with black pepper.
2. Leave to marinate for 30 minutes.
3. Brush both sides of each tomato half with olive oil, place skin side down on to rack and cook on medium until tender (about 5/8 minutes).
4. Sprinkle with extra balsamic vinegar if liked and scatter lots of torn fresh basil over the top of each tomato.
5. Chop up the olives and scatter over the top.

Vegetable Chilli

Ingredients

1 onion chopped finely
Mushrooms - chopped
2 carrots chopped
2 green chillies with seeds removed chopped
1 red chilli with seeds removed chopped
1 tea spoon of cumin & paprika
½ teaspoon of cinnamon
2 garlic cloves crushed
1 Tin of tomatoes
3 tsp of tomato puree
1 tin of red kidney beans
Oil
2 Tbsp of vinegar
1 tbsp of granulated sweetener

Instructions

1. Chop the veg and lightly fry the onion, garlic, mushrooms and whatever other veg you put in. Then add the tomato puree stir for one minute and then add the tomatoes.

2. Pour this mixture into a oven dish and add the carrot and the spices.

3. Cook for about 20 minutes on HI, then add the kidney beans vinegar and sweetener.

4. Reduce the heat and cook for a further 10 minutes. Check the carrots at this point to see whether they are tender and if not cook for further 5 minutes.

5. Serve with rice and salad.

Cheese & Potato Pie

Ingredients

2 large baking potatoes (or equivalent quantity of smaller ones), they need to be the floury sort
1 large white onion
2 large eggs
8 oz mature cheddar grated
Salt and pepper

Instructions

1. Parboil the potatoes in their skins, until just starting to soften.

2. Drain and allow to cool

3. Finely slice or chop the onion.

4. When the potatoes are cool enough to handle, thickly slice them (1/4") and place one layer (say one third of the quantity) in a greased baking dish.

5. Season with salt and pepper.

6. Add one third of the chopped onion and one third of the grated cheese.

7. Repeat the layers of seasoned potato, onion and cheese until all the ingredients are used up.

8. Beat up the eggs, pour over the potato layers and bake in oven on HI (full power) for about 40-45 minutes or until golden brown.

9. This recipe is great served with sweetcorn and petit pois

Macaroni cheese

Ingredients

75g (3oz) cooked macaroni
2 level tbsp tomato purée
1 tsp dried mixed herbs
1 packet cheese sauce mix
2 tbsp grated cheese

Instructions

1. Cooking pasta according to instructions on packet

2. Stir the tomato purée and the mixed herbs into the freshly cooked and still warm macaroni.

3. Place in an oven dish and pour (already prepared) cheese sauce and sprinkle with the grated cheese.

4. Cook for approx. 10-15 minutes on HI

Stuffed Tomatoes

Ingredients

2 beef tomatoes
Olive oil to brush
2 tbsp chopped leaf parsley
1 clove garlic, chopped
½ tbsp capers, chopped
50g (2oz) white breadcrumbs from day old bread
½ dried oregano
1 tbsp olive oil,
Salt and freshly ground black pepper

Instructions

1. Cut the tops off the tomatoes and save.

2. Scoop out the core and seed and sprinkle the inside with salt.

3. Lay cut side down on a plate and leave to drain for approx 30 minutes.

4. Brush the inside of an oven dish with olive oil.

5. Pat the inside of the tomatoes dry with kitchen paper.

6. In a small bowl mix the parsley, garlic, capers, breadcrumbs and the oregano and stir in a small tablespoon of the olive oil to bind.

7. Place in oven for 10 minutes on HI or until cooked through

8. Season to taste.

Baked celeriac

Ingredients

1 large celeriac
½ tsp sea salt
1 tbsp sweet paprika or curry powder
25g (1oz) butter
freshly ground black pepper

Instructions

1. Peel the celeriac, cut in half and cut each half into 2cm (1½") pieces.

2. Cover with sea salt and paprika or curry powder.

3. Melt the butter and add to the celeriac in an oven dish and stir to coat in the butter, season with the black pepper.

4. Cook for approx. 10 minutes, stir and cook for a further 15-20 minutes until golden brown.

5. Delicious with vegetarian sausages.

Further Information

If you would like to see more information about Halogen Cooking please visit our website www.bookshoparoundthecorner.co.uk

Or alternatively visit our blog for free recipes and advise:

www.cherrymay.com/thehalogencookbook